People Around Town

MEET THE TEACHER

By Joyce Jeffries

Gareth Stevens
Publishing

Please visit our website, www.garethstevens.com. For a free color catalog of all our high-quality books, call toll free 1-800-542-2595 or fax 1-877-542-2596.

Library of Congress Cataloging-in-Publication Data

Jeffries, Joyce.
  Meet the teacher / Joyce Jeffries.
      p. cm. — (People around town)
  Includes index.
  ISBN 978-1-4339-7341-3 (pbk.)
  ISBN 978-1-4339-7342-0 (6-pack)
  ISBN 978-1-4339-7340-6 (library binding)
  1. Teachers—Juvenile literature. I. Title.
  LB1775.J44 2013
  371.1—dc23

                                    2012008302

First Edition

Published in 2013 by
Gareth Stevens Publishing
111 East 14th Street, Suite 349
New York, NY 10003

Editor: Katie Kawa
Designer: Andrea Davison-Bartolotta

Photo credits: Cover, pp. 13, 19, 24 (library) Digital Vision/Thinkstock; p. 1 Hemera/Thinkstock; p. 5 iStockphoto/Thinkstock; p. 7 Brand X Pictures/Thinkstock; pp. 9, 24 (pencil) Juriah Mosin/Shutterstock.com; p. 11 Creatas/Thinkstock; pp. 15, 17, 24 (chalkboards) Photodisc/Thinkstock; p. 21 Nadejda Ivanova/Shutterstock.com; p. 23 Wavebreak Media/Thinkstock.

Printed in the United States of America

CPSIA compliance information: Batch #CS12GS: For further information contact Gareth Stevens, New York, New York at 1-800-542-2595.

Contents

Writing and Reading 4

A Teacher's Tools 14

Kinds of Teachers 18

Words to Know 24

Index 24

A teacher works
with a group of kids.
This is her class.

She helps them write
new words.

They write with pencils.

She helps them read
books too.

They go to a place
with a lot of books.
This is a library.

Teachers use maps.
These show different
places on Earth.

They write on boards.
These are called
chalkboards.

apple
ant
atom
anim
airplane

17

There are many kinds of teachers.

Some teach about the past. This is called history.

Some teach math.
They help kids add.

$2 + 1 = 3$

$2 + 2 = 4$

$2 + 3 = 5$

Words to Know

chalkboard   library   pencil

Index

history 20   maps 14
library 12   math 22